KA-POW TO POWERJAMS

Written by Beckie Jas
Illustrated by Brandon Koepke

Halton REGION

Oakville, Ontario

"Wake up, Biff," squawked Tyto. "You too, Alba-Alba. Today we meet our exchange students from the far north."

"Can we take them snowboarding at Glen Eden?" asked Biff.

"Sure, we can go tomorrow," said Tyto. "First, we must tidy the tree-trunk hollow for our guests."

At once, Tyto turned on all the lights and started the electric feather buster.

"Achoo!" squeaked Alba-Alba as she fired up the heateroo. It rumbled like an empty stomach.

Biff tossed a pair of socks into the tumble-drum and pressed start.

START
START
One snowflake, two snowflakes, three snowflakes, four.

A few hours later, the chores were done and the tree-trunk hollow was warm as shrew stew.

Tyto, Biff, and Alba-Alba relaxed in front of the heateroo, waiting for their new friends to arrive.

Suddenly, there was a tap, tap, tap on the tree-trunk door.
Tyto flew to answer it.

Outside there were two ginormous fluffy birds:
a Snowy Owl and a Gyrfalcon.

"You must be Quincy and Nahanni," said Tyto,
as the big birds entered the tree-trunk hollow.

Tyto quickly closed the door behind
them as snowflakes swooshed inside,
tickling their talons.

Alba-Alba gave Nahanni and Quincy a tour of the tree-trunk hollow.

"This is where we eat," said Alba-Alba.

The birds listened closely while squeezing themselves into the kitchen.

Alba-Alba hopped onto her branch bunk. "And this is where we sleep."

"Thank you for sharing your home with us," said Nahanni.

After a long and slumberous sleep, the birds woke to see a million snowflakes on the treetops—and millions more falling from the sky.

"Glen Eden, here we fly!" said Biff, as he raced around collecting snowboards, bindings, and boots.

After a hearty breakfast of rodent scramble and fried lemming, it was time to go.

But when they
opened the door,
it was

IMPOSSIBLE!

The tree-trunk hollow
was

SNOWED IN!

"It looks like a blustery blizzard followed us here from the Arctic," croaked Nahanni.

"And so did the cold air," added Alba-Alba.

Disappointed, they plopped themselves in front of the tellytube.

Suddenly, the tree-trunk hollow
went DARK...AND QUIET.

The tellytube fizzled and flickered to NOTHINGNESS.

The heateroo rocked and rumbled to SILENCE.

"Uh oh," whispered Biff. "I think we're having a powerjam."

"What do we do now?" asked Alba-Alba. "It's going to get very cold in here."

Tyto appeared with some flashlights. "Don't worry," he said. "Everything will turn back on soon."

But they waited, and waited, and waited. The snow didn't seem to care. It kept on falling, and falling, and falling.

HEATEROO
Eleven snowflakes, twelve snowflakes, thirteen snowflakes, brrr.

“You don’t need to freeze your feathers off,” said Nahanni.

“That’s right,” added Quincy. “We can show you how to stay warm and how to prepare for powerjams.”

Nahanni made a checklist and they quickly got to work.

NAHANNI'S COZY CHECKLIST:
1. Biff - get sweaters, scarves, and slippers
2. Tyto - roll blankets into draft catchers
3. Alba-Alba - find emergency kit
4. Quincy - look for a portable radio

"Where we come from, we are extra careful about how we use energy," said Nahanni.

"We turn off the lights, unplug our gadgets, and we don't blast the heateroo," explained Quincy.

"Saving energy is good for the environment," added Nahanni.

"Then we must save energy," said Tyto. "If you can do it, we can too."

Outside, the snowflakes began to fall slower and softer, like floating feathers. It was perfect for snow games.

The birds bundled up and together they shovelled their way out of the tree-trunk hollow.

They made snow birds and snow forts and then played a game of freeze tag.

An hour later, the birds returned inside for a snack: marmot and cheese and mice and beans.

Then all of a sudden—the lights, tellytube, and heateroo rumbled back on. The powerjam was over!

"KA-POW TO POWERJAMS!" shouted Alba-Alba.

"Thanks to our friends, we know how to prepare for powerjams AND how to be energy smart."

Biff was bursting with excitement. "Finally, we can go snowboarding!"

GLEN
EDEN

But—there was one small problem.

"We don't know how to snowboard," said Quincy.

"Oh!" said Tyto. "We can help you with that."

"It's like sledding on your talons," added Alba-Alba.

Nahanni flapped her wings with delight. "Now it's our turn to learn from you."

That night, they all hit the slopes together.

They flew high in the sky, then slid low in the snow—jumping, jibbing, sliding, and riding.

One jump, two jumps, three jumps, four. **KA-POW** to powerjams and powerjams no more!

DEFINITIONS

Heateroo, tumble-drum, tellytube: a furnace, a clothes dryer, a television.

Blizzard: a severe snowstorm with high winds and low visibility.

Powerjam: a power outage as a result of a shortage, downed wire, mechanical failure, or overuse by consumers.

Jibbing: a snowboarding action to jump or ride over an object.

Shrew: a small mouse-like mammal with a long pointed snout and tiny eyes.

Lemming: a small, short-tailed rodent found in the Arctic tundra.

Marmot: a heavily built, burrowing rodent of the squirrel family.

DID YOU KNOW?

- A squirrel's nest of leaves and twigs in a tree is called a "drey."
- Snowflakes come in a variety of shapes and sizes. No two snowflakes are alike.
- Powerjams can happen at any time of the year, especially during snowstorms, thunderstorms, and even heatwaves when demand for electricity is high.
- Two common asthma triggers are dust and cold outdoor air.

FACTS ABOUT ARCTIC BIRDS

Gyrfalcon (pronounced: jeer-falcon)

The scientific name for the Gyrfalcon is *Falco rusticolus*. It's an Arctic species and can be found in Northern Ontario. Gyrfalcons hunt near the ground and eat ground birds, hares, and rodents. They have long pointed powerful wings and are the largest falcon in the world, weighing up to 4.5 lbs with a 5 ft wingspan.

Snowy Owl

The scientific name for Snowy Owl is *Bubo scandiacus*. It's Ontario's heaviest owl and can weigh over 6 lbs with a 5 ft wingspan. They have broad wings and a round head without visible ear-tufts. Found in the tundra, males are white and females are white with dark spots. Snowy Owls eat shrews, lemmings, hares, and marmots.

Visit Nahanni and Quincy up close at Mountsberg Raptor Centre in Halton Region: **www.raptorcentre.ca**.

ENERGY SMART TIPS

- Install a programmable thermostat to control temperature in your home.
- Seal air leaks around windows, doors, and dryer vents.
- Turn off computers and electronics when not in use.
- In winter, keep curtains open in daytime and close them at night.
- Replace inefficient light bulbs with energy-efficient alternatives.
- Wash and rinse clothes in cold water.
- Service your furnace and clean or change filter regularly.
- Insulate water pipes and add insulation to your attic and house walls.

Saving energy reduces pollution and is good for air quality.
For more tips, visit: **www.halton.ca/airquality**.

EMERGENCY KIT CHECKLIST

Emergencies can happen at any time. It's important to be prepared (pack a three-day supply per person).

- Flashlight and batteries
- Radio and batteries or crank radio
- First-aid kit
- Candles and matches/lighter
- Extra car keys
- Cash in small amounts
- Important papers and identification
- Food, bottled water, and manual can opener
- Clothing and footwear
- Blankets or sleeping bags
- Toilet paper and personal items
- Medications
- Whistle (to attract attention, if needed)
- Playing cards, games
- Backpack to hold all emergency items
- Items for your pets

"SEEK AND FIND" ACTIVITIES

1) Can you count the 13 gigantic snowflakes in the story?

2) Can you identify two things in the story that trigger asthma?

3) Can you find Echo (a small Screech Owl) in the story?

FOR MORE INFORMATION

A Farewell to Featherwagons: **www.halton.ca/featherwagons**

Wings and Thingamajigs: **www.halton.ca/thingamajigs**

Ka-Pow to Powerjams: **www.halton.ca/powerjams**

Air Quality and Climate Change Tools for Schools:
www.halton.ca/toolsforschools

Emergency Preparedness: **www.halton.ca/beprepared**

ANSWERS: 1) Snowflakes: page 5, 7, 11, 17 **2)** Dust and cold air **3)** Page 26

Many have helped in the making of this book. A sincere thank you to the Air Quality and Climate Change Picture Book Committee: Samantha Bosworth (Registered Early Childhood Educator, Halton Region), Julia Brdarevic (Public Health Nurse, Halton Region), Sharon Campbell-Springstead (Early Literacy Specialist, Ontario Early Years, Halton Region), Amy Fennell (Raptor Centre Lead, Mountsberg Conservation Area, Conservation Halton), Carla Hanna (Health Promoter, Halton Region), Beckie Jas (Environmental Health Specialist, Halton Region), Anna Larson (Communications Specialist, Halton Region), and Peter Steer (Environmental Health Senior Policy Analyst, Halton Region).

Thank you to Walter Scattolon for the clever powerjam concept.

Thank you to Bonnie Robertson Koepke for all you do.

Book design by Brandon Koepke (www.koepke.ca)
Produced by Callawind Children's Books (www.callawind.com)
Printed and bound in Canada by Friesens (www.friesens.com)

Summary: Biff, Tyto and Alba-Alba are getting ready for visitors from the far north and are excited about taking them snowboarding. Together, they tidy their tree-trunk hollow without giving much thought to their energy use. After their guests arrive, a power failure during a winter storm delays their snowboarding plans. This gives the owls a chance to learn some valuable lessons about the importance of using energy wisely and preparing for emergencies.

Keywords: Environment, Energy Conservation, Air Quality, Climate Change, Air Pollution, Asthma, Emergency Preparedness, Raptors

Library and Archives Canada Cataloguing in Publication

Jas, Beckie
Ka-pow to powerjams / written by Beckie Jas ;
illustrated by Brandon Koepke.

Ages 4-8
ISBN 978-0-9865648-3-3

1. Electric power failures--Juvenile literature. 2. Electric power--Conservation--Juvenile literature. 3. Emergency management--Juvenile literature.

I. Koepke, Brandon II. Halton (Ont.) III. Title.

TK1010.J38 2013 333.793'216 C2013-901310-5

Halton Region
Dial 311 or 905-825-6000
Toll free 1-866-4HALTON (1-866-442-5866)
TTY 905-827-9833
www.halton.ca

Halton REGION

Access Halton
Dial 311 www.halton.ca